650 | The Sound of Music

Edited by Edward McCann

650 | WHERE WRITERS READ
Founder / Editor • Edward McCann
Executive Producer • Richard Kollath
Literary Ombudsman • Steven Lewis
Director of Operations • Jane Kaupp
Design Director • Diane Fokas
Social Media Strategist • Shayna Miller
Director of Photography • Kevin O'Connor
Chief Audio Engineer • Jesse Chason
Videography / Photography • Sara Caldwell
Copy Editor • Kathleen Stanley
Technical Advisor • Conrad Trautmann
Technical Advisor • Stephen Kaupp

Production Assistants
Robert Dennison, Lynn Dennison, Mackenzie Meeks,
Jackie Mercurio, Brian Reagher, and Isabella Fokas

Advisory Committee
Rachel Aydt, Laura Shaine Cunningham, Angela Davis-Gardner,
Karen Dukess, Joseph Goodrich, David Masello, Honor Molloy,
Irene O'Garden, John Pielmeier, Gretchen Reed, James Russek,
Angela Derecas Taylor, and Julie Trelstad

"A painter paints pictures on canvas.
But musicians paint their pictures on silence."
—*Leopold Stokowski*

ABOUT 650

Music is an ancient and international language, and it has been with us, on this planet, since the first birdsong—and likely even earlier. Music can communicate things we can't quite put into words, and in 1697, English playwright and poet William Congreve wrote that "Musick has charms to soothe a savage breast." The pieces in this anthology were first performed for a live audience in a New York City theater, and I hope this collection of finely crafted and curated personal stories about music not only soothes, but also inspires and engages you with its range of perspectives and experience.

Read650 is a celebration of writing and the spoken word, a literary forum for personal stories performed five minutes—and 650 words—at a time. Read650 events invite a range of expression, and recordings of the performances are added to a digital archive, with additional exposure through podcasts, broadcasts, our YouTube channel, and in these printed volumes.

We feature graduate students and grandparents, first-timers and bestsellers. If you love language and enjoy a good story, you've come to the right place. To submit your work or attend our shows, visit our website or Facebook page, and join our mailing list. Tell your friends about 650, and spread the word about the spoken word.

Ed McCann

Edward McCann, Founder / Editor

READ650.COM
FACEBOOK.COM/READ650

CONTENTS

650 | The Sound of Music

Edited by Edward McCann

JEREMIAH HORRIGAN

Jeremiah Horrigan has spent his professional life as a newspaper reporter telling other people's stories in several daily upstate New York newspapers, *The New York Times, Sports Illustrated, The Miami Herald* and *The Hartford Courant.* These days, he prefers to tell his own story and has done so in *salon.com, Memoir Journal, Talking Writing* and in several anthologies, including *Woodstock Revisted.* He has a bylined blog at the *Huffington Post* and has written two memoirs.

SPLANG!

Jeremiah Horrigan

I was a teenage zombie. My body was slowly being taken over by forces beyond my control. My mouth would emit weird, unexpected honking sounds when I spoke. My skin became cratered as the moon. Patches of hair sprouted from unlikely places. But the worst part of this invasion was the way it made me feel: I was a lonely teenage zombie. You would not have wanted to know me then. Especially if you were that most mysterious of creatures -- a girl.

Unable to understand my afflictions, I resolved to protect myself as best I could. I donned the mask of sarcasm. I became the Sneering One, the hypocrite who disguised his jealousy of all things good and sweet with sour mockery. And my mockery was never so acidic as when I heard my younger sister Karen play her Beatles albums. The Beatles were, after all, a girl band. No manly 14-year-old zombie would be caught dead listening to those cute, huggable visitors from another planet.

Neither Karen nor anyone else in my family suspected the truth: when everyone was asleep, I would steal into the living room and lie on the floor, my head stuck between the removable twin speakers of my parents' stereo and I would listen surreptitiously, at barely audible levels, to "Meet the Beatles," "Beatles '65" and especially the soundtrack to "A Hard Day's Night." Though I couldn't admit it to Karen, let alone myself, I was in love with The Beatles too.

A few years ago, on a sultry July afternoon, I was lying in a hospital bed, recovering from abdominal surgery, watching numbly as tendrils of depression began to creep up the legs of that sodden, unfriendly bed.

At lunchtime that day, I received not the greasy hamburger-and-fries my IV-fed body craved but something infinitely tastier: my daughter Annie's laptop.

It was there and then that I reconnected with my closeted teenage past. Without a moment's hesitation, I Googled up YouTube and punched in the words "beatles hard day's night." A blank screen gave way to that bizarre, unforgettable opening chord — SPLANG gggg — the chord that signaled the beginning of the running, jumping, standing-still opening credits of Richard Lester's great movie. A thrill ran through my battered body as I watched those grinning young men run from mobs of screaming, delirious girls.

I must have played that clip a dozen times that day. Every time I did, my hospital cell melted away, replaced by that remembered living room floor where my long-ago, skinny, secretive self again lay enraptured. When I snapped the laptop closed that evening, I felt

2

newly alive, nourished for the first time since my surgery.

There I was, nearly half a century later, tears in my eyes, resembling no one in the movie more than Paul's grandfather, knowing as much as it's possible for a clean old man to know how thrilling it must have been to have been a lovesick teenage girl back then, screaming, galloping after her favorite Beatle, sobbing at the pure mysterious pleasure of a race she knew she could never win but running it just the same. It's a passion that should never have been sneered at but treasured for the tender moment it was.

That song, that film clip, those screaming girls were as inspiring to me as any of the great freedom songs of the civil rights era. I felt utterly refreshed, ready for anything, ready to throw off my thin blanket, rip out the IV line and dash madly down the dismal hallway outside my door, down to the steamy city streets below, running, running like those girls, running away from the misery and self-pity that had nearly taken me over. It had been a hard day's night, yeah, but I'd get out of that damned hospital no matter what, I'd get home and I would feel all right.

KAREN DUKESS

Karen Dukess is the author of the novel *The Last Book Party*, to be published in July 2019 by Henry Holt & Co. She has been a tour guide in the former Soviet Union, a newspaper reporter at the *St. Petersburg Times* in Florida, and the founding features editor of *The Moscow Times* in Russia. She has written book reviews for *USAToday* and blogged about raising teen-aged boys at *theblunderyears.com* and the *Huffington Post*. Her narrative non-fiction has appeared in *Intima* (Columbia University) and her short story, "Fancy Hat," appeared in the 2017 issue of the *Westchester Review*. She is a speechwriter at UN Development Programme and is a member of the Terzo Piano writer's group. She lives in Pelham, New York.

DAVE McKENNA WAS A LEGEND

Karen Dukess

I was in my sophomore year at college when I got a surprise phone call from my father. "Want a date for Friday night?" he asked. The jazz pianist Dave McKenna would be playing at a club in Providence and my father had two tickets. He would drive up from New York and be outside my dorm at 6.

Dave McKenna was "a legend," my father had often told me.

"Just listen to his unusual sense of time," he'd said a few months earlier, after getting a new McKenna album. "Do you hear it?"

"Yup," I said, and waited for that inevitable moment when he would lift the needle from the LP and place it down ever so carefully so I could hear a particular bridge again.

Glenn Miller, Duke Ellington, Benny Goodman, Bob Wilber - my father loved them all. I heard them all, and I heard about them all, without really listening. My father's music was ancient and musty, with songs you could sing along to only by muttering "bah-

bah-baa" or "do-dah-do-do," which he never hesitated to do when one of his favorites came on the car radio.

At six o'clock, just as promised, Dad rolled up to my dorm. The jazz club was small and dark; the audience old. Slumped at the piano, McKenna was a wide-shouldered guy in a suit and tie. With thinning hair, he looked more like a washed-out insurance salesman than a legendary jazz pianist.

McKenna was impressive on the piano, but I found the music slippery, difficult to latch onto, endless. My father was enraptured.

After the second set, my Dad walked up to the piano to talk to Mr. McKenna and buy an album for me. He beamed when his idol smiled my way and autographed the cover. I thanked them both for the album, which I later slid onto a shelf in my dorm room, and never played.

Two years ago, decades after I lost track of that neglected album, my son Johnny started playing piano. His repertoire was typical for a young teenager: a lot of Billy Joel and some Beatles. It was not my father's favorite music, but he loved to listen to Johnny play anyway – even when he got too weak to come downstairs to sit by the piano.

And then this autumn, a few months after my father died, Johnny's piano teacher taught him some jazz tunes – Miles Davis and Thelonius Monk – and introduced him to Duke Ellington, Art Tatum and Dick Hyman. Johnny practiced jazz chords and riffs, learned blues scales, and started improvising, the music flowing from him with a seemingly effortless joy.

One evening, while Johnny was playing the piano and I was making dinner in the kitchen, I realized: I know this music; this is the soundtrack of my childhood.

I followed the intertwining strands of melody, and stayed with the songs as they rose and wandered and came back around again. The rhythms were intoxicating, the bridges artful. How had I not heard any of it before? Why had my father's passion for jazz – so constant and true – touched me only when he was gone?

I read in the paper recently that scientists have recorded the sound of two black holes colliding a billion light years away, and that this is evidence that space and time are interwoven, as Einstein said. I don't understand this, but I would like to believe that time rippling and bending means that when Johnny and I listen to one of my father's old Dave McKenna recordings, my father is hearing it, too, that we are all in the exact same moment, happy and slightly astonished, as the melody, and the technique, and the magic take us away.

MANUELA HOELTERHOFF

Manuela Hoelterhoff is a commentator and editor whose topics have ranged widely over the contemporary world to include opera and theater, art and architecture, literature and travel, and how animals affect our lives. Her first articles appeared in William F. Buckley's *National Review*. A twenty-year stint followed at the Wall Street Journal where she wrote reviews and served as arts editor, books editor, and member of the editorial board. won the annual Pulitzer Prize for Criticism, citing "her wide-ranging criticism on the arts and other subjects." A founding editor of *SmartMoney* magazine, she also worked with Harold Evans to create *Condé Nast Traveler*. Most recently, she served as an executive editor and columnist for *Bloomberg News* and was named a Guggenheim Fellow for her forthcoming book, *Hitler's Summer Seasons*.

DREAMING IN THE DARK

Manuela Hoelterhoff

Seated way up in the Family Circle at the Metropolitan Opera I looked down on two round people in costumes from a distant era. What are they singing about? I asked my mother. Eternal love, she whispered. Read your program.

To the extent I had any deeper understanding of love in my teens, it seemed that love was reserved for beautiful people, say fleet-footed quarterbacks, thin blonde prom queens and movie stars. Zinka Milanov and Richard Tucker, the leads in Giordano's "Andrea Chenier," were neither young nor fair, and yet when they embraced, the intensity of their duet transcended the reality of their appearance. By the time they climbed toward the guillotine I was enslaved.

Back in Valley Cottage, New York, our house was small and crowded, stuffed with Salvation Army furniture and a few boxes of souvenirs and photo albums from the life my parents left behind in Germany and Latvia. During the Second World War my mother had migrated from Riga to Berlin where she worked as a translator in the offices of the dumb and nasty Foreign Minister Joachim von Ribbentrop. My father, an officer in the Wehrmacht, was a chauffeur assigned to Field Marshal Wilhelm Keitel--later also executed at Nuremberg -- before being dispatched to Russia as a tank commander. In one of the boxes I opened after his death I found tiny black and white photographs of his long and increasingly dismal journey from Poland into the Soviet Union. He ground to a halt outside Stalingrad where most of his comrades in the Sixth Army froze to death.

Nobody talked much. I was the only child of parents brought together by the deaths of partners they mourned and they had little in common. My father raised mute creatures like fish and turtles; my educated mother played opera highlights on the one handsome piece we owned, a polished Grundig record player, which she soon blemished with a cigarette burn.

At the opera, where everything was grandly scaled, I was swept into a world of mystery and beauty so different from my everyday existence in blue-collar suburbia that I spent as much time in the dark as possible. Weekends were great when the Met played matinees and evenings on Saturday and the City Opera performed twice on Sunday.

Instead of ending up working for the phone company or a pet store, I got ambitious and look back on a satisfying career in arts journalism at the Wall Street Journal and Bloomberg News. I wrote an opera libretto, "Modern Painters" set to music by David Lang, a book about Cecilia Bartoli, ``Cinderella & Company," and just now I am finishing ``Hitler's Summer Seasons: Backstage With the Fuhrer." Yes, Adolf also loved sitting in the dark. He especially loved the epic works of Richard Wagner. Otto Dietrich, his flabbergasted press representative, thought he may have seen ``Die Meistersinger von Nurnberg'' one hundred times. There are so many mastersingers in Wagner's Nuremberg that the opera is about six hours long. So that's a lot of sitting in the dark. The Fuhrer spent at least a week every summer at the Bayreuth Festival where any composer but Wagner is verboten. He was extremely knowledgeable and knew the operas by heart, especially ``Gotterdammerung,'' the last of the four-opera ``Ring'' cycle which ends with the world destroyed by fire.

After defeating France in the summer of 1940, Hitler immediately left for Bayreuth to see ``Twilight of the Gods.'' He never attended another opera, not there, not anywhere. Now that the world was his stage and his to burn, Hitler had no need for little Bayreuth or any other operatic substitute.

It's disturbing to contemplate, but his dreaming in the dark made me and my own dreams possible.

JOHN GREDLER

John Gredler, poet and memoirist, is a frequent contributor to 650 who's been writing in notebooks and journals for most of his adult life. He honed his craft at the Writing Institute at Sarah Lawrence College, Bella Villa Writers, 125, and the Terzo Piano Workshops. A recipient of the 2014 Gurfein Fellowship from The Writing Institute at Sarah Lawrence College, John's work has been published in *Atticus Review, Fictionique, Narratively, Dan's Papers, Westchester Review,* and *Talking Writing.* John lives and writes in Tuckahoe, New York.

SING FOR THE MOMENT

John Gredler

Ann and I are sitting outside a little pizza place waiting for our son to join us. He is getting his hair cut before going to the local fair. The sun is low, the sky a pale mottled blue, on the horizon smudges of mauve and yellow. After a while Liam ambles up to us, hair very short, three stripes cut into one side. The barber charges a dollar each for those.

At home he carries his radio into the bathroom and blasts rap music while he showers. This a recent annoyance, he cranks up the volume without concern for what we might be doing. When he is finished we smell cologne wafting down the stairs. He puts on baggy shorts and a tight black tee, a heavy silver chain with crucifix around his neck. His present for his fourteenth birthday, the one he bothered us about for months prior.

I drop him off at the CVS parking lot, a group of girls and boys waiting. 'Hello Mr. Gredler' some of them call out, bouncing on tip toe, excited at being who they are.

I don't go home right away. I keep driving because the music
is good on the radio. Neil Young singing 'After the Gold Rush'. I'm
not sure why but the song always gets to me, something beyond the
lyrics, his plaintive voice, a sadness embodied there. My eyes fill with
tears.

Patches of kids are walking to the fair, a group of four boys all
wearing short sleeve plaid shirts in various colors and patterns. A
clutch of long hairs dressed in black on skateboards. Three tall skinny
guys walking awkwardly in white tees and gym shorts. Behind
them a group of girls in short shorts and snug shirts, all holding cell
phones with different colored cases.

The sky is now pastel pink, then purplish gray as it turns to
dusk. A bruise.

Later, when Liam returns from the fair he asks me if I want
to go sit in Ann's new car and listen to music. He is surprised when
I say yes. He ramps up the volume as we listen to Eminem's 'Sing
for the Moment' remix. I am moved by the song and wonder if it is
Liam's way to say he wants to understand something of who I am,
how my father leaving when I was a boy affected me.

I cringe at some of the harsh language, and wonder if I am
remiss to even allow Liam to listen, but I am struck by Eminem's
honesty, and by how he mixed Aerosmith's 'Dream On' into his
poem. I feel the raw truth of his words. As we listen I think I never
wanted to punch my father as in the lyrics. My anger wasn't like that.
Yet perhaps it would have been better if I had hit him rather then to
hold onto the pain of betrayal and turn it back on him for so many

years. The guitar riff at the end of the song lifts me.

When 'Mockingbird' comes on Liam sings along, knowing every word. Then he plays Jay Z's 'Death of Autotune' at my request. I like the jazz in it, the movement of the horns.

I remember sitting like this next to my father as a boy and later as a man. The smell of his cologne mixed with leather and cigarette smoke, being so physically near each other in that closed space, both of us looking ahead through the windshield.

I am stunned to be sitting in the car next to my son, listening to the music he loves, the moon in front of us setting into clouds above the trees, a pale white stain.

FELICE NEALS

Felice Neals lives in New York City, where she is pursuing her MFA in Creative Writing at City College, CUNY. Neals is working on a novel and a series of personal essays and, as an avid traveler, she often uses her adventures as the inspiration for her work. Her short story, "The Crossing," was recently published by Day One, Amazon's literary journal, and she recently received the Silver Award for Adventure Travel by the Solas Awards for travel writing.

She received her MA in Media/Film studies from The New School University and has written three screenplays.

ROCK STAR LOVE CHILD

Felice Neals

I was fourteen and had just finished the unauthorized biography. It was clear that I was the third illegitimate child of Jimi Hendrix.

Jimi was tall. So was I. Jimi was musical. So was I. Jimi loved Mozart, so did I. And … my arms were like the spitting image of his.

My mother was also in London a lot around the time that Jimi died.

I'd always loved his music. My Uncle John (who'd seen Maria Callas three times at the La Scala Opera House in Rome, I'm sure he'd like me to add), would play his albums constantly—*Live at Monterey, Band of Gypsys, Live at the Filmore East, The Cry of Love*—well after Jimi's passing; and he schooled me on the brilliant riffs of Jimi's guitar.

I started to ask my mother questions about her time abroad, about when she'd met my father, and when exactly she was in London when Jimi was playing.

In the bio it clearly stated that Jimi had—quote: affairs with several women concurrently before his untimely death—unquote. Anything was possible. It was the all the proof I needed.

My uncle was the only one I could talk to. I said, "Uncle John, is it true?"

He smiled and said, "Why do you want to be the unclaimed child of a rock star?"

I told him that it chose me. That I was destined to be the offspring of someone who dwelled in the beat of a 4/4 meter with a snare drum back beat.

After that, I stayed up many nights thinking that I should write to my siblings, his other children, Tamara Hendrix and James Sundquist. I wanted to ask if they'd heard about a third child. A love child who was ferreted off to the genteel suburbs of New Jersey. But something stopped me.

Instead, I took guitar lessons. The teacher said that the guitar was not my strong suit. I should try piano lessons, I had the hands for it. I said, Do you know who I am??

Then I tried to write songs. But the words didn't come.

I wrote a poem:

Jimi's strum. Chuck Berry's Leap.
Keep me strong with every beat.

When I ponder my demise.

Being judged through doubtful eyes.

I keep the rhythm in my heart. And know my dream will never part.

(I never said that I was Maya Angelou's daughter.)

My Uncle told my parents about my suspicions. They apparently laughed and said, "Well, if she wants to believe that she is Jimi Hendrix's daughter, what can we do?"

A part of me still believes that I am Jimi's love child. And that part of me, the unclaimed part of me, is still seeking the answers. 'Cause as my dad said:

"But you and I we've been through that

And this is not our fate

So let us not talk falsely now

The hour's getting late."

LAWRENCE WINTERS

Lawrence Winters is a poet, novelist, playwright, combat Marine, group psychotherapist, wood-artist, husband, and Black Peace Eagle. His first book, *The Making and Unmaking of a Marine*, is a memoir about how a child is forged into a recruit for the Marines, his subsequent journey to war, and his return to Vietnam many years later to speak about his sins and ask forgiveness.

Larry's second book, *Brotherkeeper*, is a novel that delves into an untold dimension of war, beyond physical and emotional injury, called moral wounding. Currently, he's writing a novel entitles, *The Wren* that plumbs the aftereffects of war on families, enemies, children, and an indifferent public.

THE HYMN

Lawrence Winters

November 20, 1967, Marine boot camp Parris Island North Carolina. With seventy-two Marines on the rifle range, drill instructor Gunny Webb yelled, "platoon halt." The platoon stood at ease in the shade of live oaks, Gunny paced and said, "Soon you'll be close to calling yourselves Marines. Then like me, when you hear the Marine Hymn the hair on your neck will stand. There's no greater honor than giving your life for your country. Girls that's ain't gonna happen if you don't hit the friggin' targets. Attention, forward, march, you move like a herd of sheep. The scores will improve, or we'll find some motivation."

Gunny whispered, "Platoon, halt!" Only a few men heard him and stopped; the men who didn't bumped and tumbled into each other. "You march like girls. Attention, order arms, port arms, right shoulder arms, inspection arms." He spit the commands. Gunny drilled us so long I felt my arm muscles snapping over my shoulder bones. "Girls, feel the weapon like it's part of your body. Stack arms!" Walking between ranks inspecting tripods of weapons, Gunny stood in front me, put his mouth to my ear, "Retrieve your weapon, Turd."

I reached for my rifle, making the men next to me grab theirs. My safety was off.

Gunny's broad brim was in my face. I fingered my safety. Gunny roared, "Present Arms!" It scared me so I couldn't respond.

"Present arms, you damn worm!" Gunny's arm shot out like a rattlesnake grabbing my rifle by the barrel. He flung it into the dirt.

"Retrieve your rifle, Turd!" Sand streamed out the barrel.

"Give me your weapon," he said, sitting on an ammo box. Snatching it he laid it across his knees.

"Come here, Boy. Pull back the operating rod."

I did. The sand scratched, and the bolt locked.

"Put your thumb in the chamber."

I screamed inside, *You crazy bastard!*

"Release the bolt, boy!"

The spring tension of an M-14 is fourteen pounds. My finger trembled releasing the bolt. The bolt drove into my thumbnail. My arm jerked spasmodically making the bolt dig deeper into my thumb. I saw the platoon standing at attention.

"Pay attention, turd. Pull the trigger." "I hate you," I mouthed.

"Pull the trigger, damn it!" "Yes sir," I hesitated.

A falsetto scream, "Pull the trigger now or you'll be putting your private part in that chamber!"

I pulled the trigger and the firing pin entered my thumbnail.

Pain raced the bones of my arm like I'd stuck my thumb in an electrical outlet.

My rifle sat on Gunny's lap. My tears dripped off my cheeks onto his trousers. I tasted blood from my teeth buried in my lower lip. All I could see was Gunny's neck. I knew in seconds I'd kill him. Not he, or the entire platoon could stop me.

"Stand up, worm." I straightened, lifting the rifle off his lap. The pain forced my eyes closed.

"Stand at attention, turd, March out there in front of my girls. Show them your filthy rifle." He stood hands on his hips.

"Halt, turd! Sing my girls the Marine Corps Hymn."

I was aware then he knew when I'd break better than I did. I reached to support the rifle dripping my blood from the barrel.

"Let it hang freely, boy. You jeopardized my girls' lives."

I staggered in front of the platoon, not meeting their eyes. All of them knew it could have been them.

"Turd, I want to hear the sound of music, now!"

The words stuck. "From the Halls of Montezuma to the shores of Tripoli."

"We can't hear you, worm!"

"From...the H-h-h--halls of Montezuma, to the shores of Tripoli; we will f-f-fight our country's battles, in the air, on land, and sea..."

Tiptoeing, to not jounce the rifle, I sang. Each spike of pain my voice got louder until I bellowed. Between my breaths, I could hear the platoon singing with me, and I felt the hair on my neck stand.

STEVEN LEWIS

Steven Lewis, Literary Ombudsman for 650, is a columnist at *Talking Writing*, and a member of the Sarah Lawrence College Writing Institute faculty. A longtime freelancer, his work has been published in *The New York Times, The Washington Post, Christian Science Monitor, the Los Angeles Times, Ploughshares, Spirituality & Health* and others. Recent novels include *Take This, Loving Violet,* and *A Hard Rain*, all from Codhill Press, and Finishing Line Press published Steve's poetry chapbook, *If I Die Before You Wake*. His backlist includes *Zen and the Art of Fatherhood, The ABCs of Real Family Values, The Complete Guide for the Anxious Groom,* and *Fear and Loathing of Boca Raton (a Hippie's Guide to the New Sixties)*. He divides his time between his writing space in New Paltz, New York and Hatteras Island, North Carolina.

THE SONGS IN MY HEART

Steven Lewis

I'm alone in the living room, CNN muted, shameless politicians flickering across the screen, a sweating glass of Jim Beam in my hand, and the most depressing Leonard Cohen song ever composed ("Sisters of Mercy") playing in my head. With each moment I am sinking deeper into the couch, glassy eyed, worrying about one kid and then another and then another until I am sure all seven are doomed; and then I start obsessing about work, unpaid property taxes, my wife coughing upstairs through a rib-breaking pneumonia ... when my daughter Addie phones to say she's in labor. Her fourth. Our fifteenth grandchild.

Forgive the Laura Nyro reconstruction: One more high chair at the long table. One more life-giving breath of that baby scent. One more round of "She'll be comin' round the mountain ...," and suddenly I'm humming Shades of Blue's 1964 "So in Love."

I mean, thank the stars for babies. They make your heart sing.

So I kiss my teary wife good-bye (first birth she's missed), hop in the car, the dark clouds part, the giant moon rises as big as a pizza pie ("… that's amore"), and I drive off to Yale-New Haven, cranking up Whitesnake's "Here I Go Again."

And with that ancient 8-track calling me back in time and circumstance, 2010 soon enough becomes 1987 and …

I am picking up Addie and her friend Tiffany from Andy B's 13th birthday party. Think "Mony Mony" by Billy Idol. They jump in the back seat and I ask offhandedly, like the cool dad I am, if they had a good time.

"It was great," says that familiar snarky voice I know so well, followed by a three-second pause, "… we played spin the bottle."

Tiffany squeals and giggles hand-over-mouth while I go into my Zen-dad mode: take a deep cleansing breath, Pop, don't forget to stop at the stop sign, say, 'That's nice.'

"Thaaaat's nice," I say in my coolest Lou Reed monotone.

"Yeah," she says, waiting for me to glance in the rear view mirror, her eyes big, beautiful and sparkling blue … mine murky green. Then she adds with a smirk, "and I tried French kissing."

Judging by the snorting and honking coming out of Tiffany, I figure she's seconds away from peeing on my Vanagon seats … which are saved only by, yes, another well-designed pause from my impertinent daughter, who says: "… but I didn't like it."

The 8-track memory tape clicks and stops there.

So, clock on the wall spinning ahead like in 1940s movie musicals, I am back in the more recent past tense, driving off to Connecticut, now thinking about how life was often like that—and more—with the beautiful vivacious, contentious, outrageous Adelyn Patricia Lewis.

By the time I arrive at Yale New Haven Hospital, Marguerite Lily Pietrosanti, 6lbs 15oz., has already had her first yowl and is cradled in her beautiful mother's arms, and as I glance down through my tears I see … a vivacious, contentious, outrageous smirk on that gorgeous tiny one hour old face.

And suddenly the Mormon Tabernacle Choir is belting out "Amen!" through the hospital PA system, a troop of tap dancing orderlies bursts through the door, two nurses pull back the curtains covering the plate glass window for all to see … the Connecticut hills alive with the sound of musical karma.

ART BELL

Art Bell had a long career in television beginning at CBS followed by HBO, where he founded Comedy Central. After Comedy Central, he went on to be President of Court TV. Prior to his television career, he was an economist in Washington, DC. Art lives in Larchmont, New York with his wife, Carrie. He is currently writing a memoir about Comedy Central, and playing piano and drums.

MY BIGGEST FAN

Art Bell

"Good afternoon and thank you for coming to our piano recital." My piano teacher, Dr. Rudnytsky, the aging (but still dashing) Ukrainian composer who had conducted great orchestras in Europe, welcomed the crowd of parents to his living room in Toms River, NJ. "I'm sorry it's so hot in here. Please use the programs we handed out to fan the person next to you." The audience laughed politely. I wondered if my mother was among those laughing, knowing how seriously she took my musical education. She was, after all, a piano teacher, and even without saying so, she hoped my performance that day would be exceptional, or so I imagined. I wiped the sweat off the back of my neck. Twenty-two other kids stood in the kitchen with me, uncomfortable in ties and jackets, skirts and dresses, waiting to play the pieces we'd learned. Marie, my recital partner, glanced at me nervously from across the kitchen.

Soon I heard Dr. Rudnytsky say, "Next, Marie Stoka and

Artur Bell, fourth graders, will play a sonatina for two pianos." His Ukrainian accent made my name "Our-tour."

Marie and I sat down at the side-by-side grand pianos and placed our music on the piano. I listened for the silence that always filled the moment before I started to play. Instead, I heard the low, droning sound of a fan, the pitch rising and falling like a very slow trill. I felt a breeze on the left side of my face. The offending floor fan, standing behind Marie, was blowing a gale across the room. The fan turned the page of my music. I turned it back. The page turned again. Then the pages started to flutter. Marie watched with eyes wide and mouth ajar. The audience stared at us as if paralyzed. Nobody moved to help.

I looked around for something to anchor the music-- a brick, an ashtray, some chewing gum. There was nothing on the piano, not even the usual layer of dust. I checked my pockets. Empty. I rose, walked over to the fan and calmly examined it. I couldn't find a switch, so I bent down and yanked out the plug. The undulating sound of the fan faded to silence. My music stopped rattling. I sat down and we began the piece. After finishing Marie and I took our bow. I felt the applause wash over us and allowed myself a smile.

An hour later, after the last student took his bow, Dr. Rudnytsky invited everyone to stay for coffee and cake. All the kids hurried into the dining room. The parents wandered in looking hot and tired. I saw my mother chatting in a group. I walked over and stood close to her side. Another women said, "You played very well, young man," then walked off to find her kid.

"Did I do okay?" I asked my mother. I searched her face, damp with sweat, for signs of approval, but I realized she seemed annoyed.

"My God, Arthur, why did you turn off the fan! Are you crazy?'

"But my music, it was blowing around. I had to."

"Well, you could have turned it back on when you finished. We were dying—it's probably 90 degrees in there!" I walked away, fighting back tears. Dr. Rudnytsky was standing nearby; I turned so he wouldn't see me.

"Artur," he called after me. "You played well. Very good job." I turned to him and he smiled. "And good move unplugging the fan. Just what I would have done."

"Thanks, Dr. Rudnytsky," I said, hoping he meant it.

He put his hand on my shoulder and said, "When you are on stage, sometimes you have to think fast, and you did. Good job, Artur, good job." I turned back to look at my mother, hoping she was watching and listening, but she was still with her group, facing away. I decided to go outside and sulk. Just then Mrs. Rudnytsky called out, "Come, children, I have ice cream here ..." and all the kids scrambled for their reward. Marie, rushing by me, turned and said, "C'mon Arthur, ice cream!" so I joined the line.

ELIZABETH PRIMAMORE

Elizabeth Primamore studied playwriting at HB Studio. *Just Fine* and *Blank* have been produced in HB's Ten Minute Play Festivals. *Just Fine* was published in Literature and Gender (Longman, 2010) and New America (Autumn House Press, 2012). Craig Lucas and Jack Hofsiss provided dramaturgical support for her full-length play, *Undone*, which has received readings at The Flea, The Cherry Lane, and Ensemble Studio Theatre. *Our First Christmas* and *A Child's Best Interest* have been included in a number of short play festivals. In July 2016, she was a fellow at The Virginia Center for the Creative Arts. Her most recent play, *The Professor and Michael Field*, has achieved the status of semifinalist for the 2017 Eugene O'Neill National Playwrights Conference. Elizabeth lives in New York.

SELLING MY STRAT

Elizabeth Primamore

When I was in high school, playing rock guitar was for boys, not girls. Sleater-Kinney, Bikini Kill and the riot grrrl movement were non-existent. The boys commanded the stage; the girls, bar stools. Everyone knew girls "couldn't play." Yet the wild abandon of the music, the suspension in another universe, the rebellious defiance, still seduced me like a hot lover. I got a guitar I could hardly play and my girlfriends and I formed a garage band—in our case, a living room band. We were the "perfect" ensemble of guitar, bass, keyboards, and drums.

A neighborhood boy band invited us to a jam session. I was so excited, until I got there. Amid the deafening distortion of a bad version of "Whole Lotta Love," the guitarist cranked his Marshall amp up to the max and spilled his Jimmy Page licks all over me. I could barely hear myself through my little practice amp I brought along, never mind fire off any competing licks. It didn't matter. All

I could squeeze out of my red Fender Stratocaster guitar were bar chords anyway. On the way home my mother's words clanged in my ears, "You're deaf with crooked hands." Indeed the goddess of music did not favor me.

Flash forward to CBGBs, six years later, where I went on a date with an attorney my mother was novena-ing every saint, Jesus, and Mary, for me to marry. For him, it was a lark, a night when he could let loose by shedding his professional demeanor, act the fool. He achieved his goal. Standing at the bar, he looked ridiculous in tails and top hat that he wore to look "hip" among the pink hair, torn T-shirts, and pierced lips. I didn't fare much better, standing there, sipping a seltzer. I feared an uninvited splash from the obligatory beer slugging going on around me might ruin my haute couture, lavender-flowered, chiffon dress.

Just then a band of skinny women with attitude took the stage. They played their hearts out with only bar chords. At that moment the rock 'n roll dreams that were buried deep inside me awakened, radiating to the tips of my finger and toes. Fired up, my senses blurred in a whirlwind of heat. Wow, I could do that. No wonder why a few years before I was bored stiff at that jazz fusion John McLaughlin Mahavishnu Orchestra concert. All those notes, the ultimate bombardment of tedium. After that night on The Bowery, I saw my lawyer a few more times, met his parents for dinner at a fancy French restaurant, then he disappeared. I was free.

Despite a tin ear, hardly any natural inclination, and a secret desire to be a writer, I took guitar lessons, not for fun, but with a view to a career in rock n'roll. Luckily I fell in love with a singer/poet who became my collaborator.

Our duo, "Run Girl Run," had a record produced by Mark Kamins of Madonna fame. "Angel and the Drunken Gods" and "Presents of "Mind, " our bands, played CBGBs weekly. Almost we got there, but no cigar. And oh, yeah, with 10,000 hours of practice, I mastered the guitar.

JENNY BINH BENDER

For the past fifteen years, **Jenny Binh Bender** has worked as a literacy consultant, teaching writing in elementary and middle schools while also working as a freelance editor and curriculum writer. She's the author of *The Resourceful Writing Teacher* (Heinemann, 2007) and *Teaching Young Writers to Craft Realistic Fiction* (Scholastic, 2011). In her spare time, she writes memoir, young adult fiction and the occasional poem. You can read about her recent journey through breast cancer on her blog *Writing the Wave* at WritingBreastCancer. com. Jenny is currently collaborating with another artist to interview and photograph Muslims in their community with the aim of educating non-Muslims and challenging the rise of Islamophobia. Jenny lives in Northampton, MA with her husband and two young children.

PILGRIMAGE

Jenny Binh Bender

I don't need to tell you / what it is about / you just start on the inside / and work your way out.   —*Ani Difranco*

When I close my eyes and jump, I land in a hotel in Nairobi, eleven in the morning and sleeping off my jetlag; two in the afternoon and trying to sleep off my fear; five in the evening and talking to myself in the mirror. "What were you thinking, coming here by yourself?" My image stares back at me: shaved head, brown eyes with nineteen years of searching in them, a strength I only suspect I have. But I know why I am here. I slip on my walkman so Ani Difranco can solidify my reserve: I have to act just as strong as I can / just to preserve a place / where I can be who I am. I am here to find who I am.

Next morning, I am braver than any ordinary person. I leave the hotel my mother insisted on for my first night and search for hostels. I am the only white face, the only girl from America walking these streets alone. I know Ani's lyrics by heart and cling to them like a mantra: Self preservation / is a full time occupation / I'm determined / to survive on this shore.

How scared I was then—yet fearless. Twenty years later, do I still have the courage to fly to Africa by myself? I have a different kind of strength now, I know this. I don't avert my eyes anymore in a man's world ... I played the powerless/in too many dark scenes. Still, I miss the abandon of my youth.

I miss sleeping in a row of cots and not minding that there are no walls between me and the stranger from Australia and the stranger who traveled the Nile with little more than his camera. I miss the night we all went to the bar up the road, and you, Mission, my South African love-to-be, accidentally knocked the glasses off my face. Was that the night we arranged to sleep side by side on the porch of Ma Roche's Hostel? I know Ani rang in my ears, a song for every piece of this journey: I wonder what you look like / under your T-shirt / I wonder what you sound like / when you're not wearing words / I wonder what we have / when we're not pretending. I know we talked, then we stopped talking, then we wondered, silently, whether there would be any kissing.

Yes, there was kissing. Then there was Lamu and falling in love. Lamu where we rented the three story, open-aired house for $3 a week. Where we made love in rooms with no ceiling; then, wrapped in sheets in the kitchen, you named me your Little Roman. Ani came with me there, too: We're all citizens of the womb / before we subdivide / into sexes and shades / this side / that side. I felt liberated by our lack of a shared culture. Without rules, I could be my truest self. Maybe I'd finally discover who that was.

I know I discovered the weight of your hand as we walked past donkeys and children with skin the color of clay toward rocky sand; then sand the color of clouds and about as soft, too. Later, when I visited you in London, we reminisced about the ocean. But what I've always remembered most from that island is the feeling of my heart flying open. I'm imagining your frame / every angle / and every plane / I'm imagining your smell / the one that mingled with mine.

I remember feeling full of possibility. I am a work in progress / dressed in the fabric of a world unfolding/offering me intricate patterns of questions ... / and strengths that you still haven't seen.

I remember feeling loveable for the first time in my life. It would be years, still, before I learned to love myself, but here was the beginning of finding what I was looking for.

Works Cited

DiFranco, Ani. "Talk to Me Now," "The Slant," "Work Your Way Out," "Every Angle." Ani DiFranco. Righteous Babe Records, 1990. CD.

MARGARITA MEYENDORFF

Margarita Meyendorff (Mourka) is the author of the memoir *DP: Displaced Person.* The daughter of a Russian Baron, she was born displaced, far from the opulence of Imperial Russia that was her birthright. A series of wars destroyed this privileged existence, and Margarita's life became a series of extraordinary moves. She has performed as an actress, dancer, musician, and storyteller at venues throughout the United States and in Europe.

NUTCRACKER SWEETS

Margarita Meyendorff

It was 1961, and I was entering puberty and madly, miserably in love with Rudolf Nureyev. I saw us as soulmates and rebels. We had so much in common: He was a peasant from Siberia who had leapt to fame with the Kirov Ballet and defected at the airport in Paris. I was fourteen, an immigrant rebelling against my parents in Nyack, New York. I too wanted to defect. Yet, what were the chances we would ever meet? The thought that Nureyev would never know me, made me weep, even as I gazed at the poster of him flying past in the grandest of jetes.

When my best friend, Galina's parents (also Russian emigres) bought tickets to see Nureyev at the Metropolitan Opera in New York City, I tied myself to the piano and promised my parents years of practice if they would just let me go to the show with Galina. By some God given miracle, my father acquiesced.

The date arrived. I was going to see Nureyev in the Nutcracker at the Met. We took our seats and along with hundreds of people in the audience, were soon mesmerized by Nureyev's leaps, his cat-like movements, and his sensual pas de deux, which surpassed even my highest expectations. He was beyond human. He was feline, sexual—those arched thighs, those full lips, those high cheekbones … I had to get closer … not only to Nureyev … but to being a star.

I was not without credits: When I was seven years old, I had performed as a rooster, complete with a huge red-feathered tail that swung as I moved. I had appeared front and center in a Russian Christmas play on a stage in New York City and sung the Russian equivalent of "cock a doodle doo" (Ky Ka Ри Ky) that had to conclude in a high C. I looked down at the front row, at five black-bearded Russian priests. They scared me, made me feel I would fail. I hit the note anyway. The Russian Orthodox priests' mouths flew open in a collective gasp, a minute pause, and then, the concert hall had burst out in applause and cheers. I had stood there, resplendent in my red and gold feathers, my plumy tail erect. I basked in the applause; the clapping went on and on. In that moment, I felt loved. I felt loved for being seven, loved for hitting the right note, loved without reservation; and like Nureyev, I was swept up in the moment—a moment I never left. We were right for each other and it was only a matter of time.

At the Nutcracker curtain call, the audience, in mad abandon, jumped to their feet. During the pandemonium, Galina grabbed my arm and we ran and ducked behind the curtain and found ourselves backstage in the midst of fantasyland—snowflake ballerinas, uniformed soldiers, fairies, mice, Russian, Chinese, Arab and Spanish dancers ...

Speaking in Russian, we pretended that we belonged. A dancer in harlequin tights led us to Nureyev's dressing room. After what seemed an eternity, Nureyev emerged, as magnificent as on stage - his cat-like eyes looked into mine, those sensuous lips spoke — to me. We exchanged some breathless pleasantries in Russian. "Какие вы прекрасные!" "How magnificent you are," he had said.

Nureyev seemed thrilled to meet two fourteen-year-old girls, and invited us to accompany him to his limousine. As we left by the stage door, the three of us were greeted by a crowd waiting to get a glimpse of him. Galina and I were the blessed. I had him by the right arm and Galina by the left. Before disappearing into his limousine, Nureyev leaned over and kissed each of us on the cheek. My cheek burned, with the imprint of his lips and I was branded forever — with the promise of a blazing future: Romance, stardom, love would all be mine.

EDWARD McCANN

Edward McCann is an award winning writer/producer and the founder and editor of *Read650*, celebrating the spoken word with live events in New York City and throughout the tri-state area. A longtime contributing editor to *Country Living*, his features and essays have been published in many literary journals, anthologies, and national magazines, including *Better Homes & Gardens, Good Housekeeping, The Irish Echo, The Sun,* and others. His essay, "Pregnant Again," was selected for the anthology, *Listen To Your Mother*, published by Penguin, and he's recently completed a memoir about the search for his missing nephew. He lives and writes in a pastoral spot about eighty miles north of New York City, and is at work on a collection of essays about life in the Hudson Valley.

REQUIEM

Edward McCann

Crouched before a cold fireplace with a lit match in my hand, I touched the flame to some crumpled newspaper tucked beneath the kindling, and a small headline on an adjacent page caught my eye: "College and Community Chorale to Resume." On impulse, I rescued that page and smoothed it flat on the floor. The fire crackled and roared to life as I read about a student choral group at the local college that welcomed community members—no auditions required. Rehearsals for a spring performance of Mozart's Requiem were about to begin—a three-hour class meeting for the next fifteen Wednesday nights.

I couldn't possibly do that, I thought, yet I hesitated to return the paper to the fire. The same impulse made me flag my calendar for the first class.

Though I had once loved choral singing, I catalogued all the reasons why I should just forget about this: other than some

Christmas caroling, I hadn't sung in a chorus or choir in thirty years; I'd hardly touched a keyboard or guitar or even read a piece of sheet music in nearly as long. Besides, my work schedule was too demanding and unpredictable for me to make all those rehearsals.

I was still thinking this that late winter Wednesday as I walked into the music department's Recital Hall. All was instantly familiar: the water fountain and bulletin board, the scent of floor wax, and the sounds from a distant rehearsal room: a solo piano, a woman singing scales.

Feeling like an imposter, I signed out a copy of the bound, eighty page score, took a seat in the bass section at the rear of the room, and greeted the men around me. I counted fifty singers in the room, equally split between students and gray hairs like me. While the last stragglers arrived I opened the score and began reading. I was nervous. My armpits were damp. But I calmed myself recalling my beloved elementary school music teacher, Mrs. Diane Jacobs, who taught me "Every Good Boy Does Fine."

The accompanist, a small, bald man, settled himself on the bench before the baby grand in the front of the room. The director managed a perfunctory greeting and directed us to a page somewhere in the middle of the score.

"Okay," he said, raising his hand, "Sopranos."

The pianist played, and the women up front sang as if they already knew the piece. Staring at the music, I struggled to orient myself, to follow along as the women sang.

"Now," the director said, looking toward us, "Basses."

The piano again, then the collective intake of breath around me, followed by the sound of men singing, a resonance I felt in my chest. All those notes looked like birdshot scattered on the page. Still wondering if I should really have sat with the tenors, I found my place and joined in. But when that line ended I couldn't find the next bass clef fast enough, and they went on without me.

I can't do this I thought after rehearsal, certain I wouldn't return. I felt unaccountably angry, and it seemed to me I'd been angry every day for the six months since my brother George had died—prematurely and unnecessarily in my opinion—anger that had shielded me from the grief that lurked just beneath it.

But I did return, fourteen more times, clocking nearly fifty hours singing a four-hundred-year-old funeral mass in Latin; a piece of music that's now become part of my DNA. Throughout all those hours of rehearsal, I was grieving, and I was singing that requiem for my lost brother. Those Wednesday night rehearsals had begun in the dark, but as winter receded, the days grew longer—and brighter.

The evening of the recital, finally on stage in tuxedos and gowns, we sang Mozart's masterwork beside a twenty-six piece orchestra, all of us joining to form a complex machine assembled just this one time to make an extraordinary and beautiful sound.

And then, before I knew it . . . it was spring.

DOUG MOTEL

Writer/Performer **Doug Motel** was born and raised in Atlantic City, New Jersey and performed his unique brand of thought-provoking humor in virtually all of New York's comedy clubs and in funky downtown spaces throughout the 1980s. Mr. Motel is the award-winning author of several solo plays including *Mick In America, Mind Salad,* and *Shiva Arms.* His solo play Praestigum features the stories of Judas, Benedict Arnold, and James Wormley Jones, the first African American undercover agent for the FBI. *Shiva Arms* is Motel's tour-de-force performance—the one-man show he wrote in which he portrays eleven colorful characters, from a punk rocker and a "B" movie actress to a crusty 86 year-old retired negative cutter—a dysfunctional group of tenants in a run-down Hollywood apartment building.

THE SMELL OF THE GREASEPAINT

Doug Motel

It is 1974. I am twelve years old. I am on my way to my first audition. It is a production of The Roar of the Greasepaint and the Smell of Crowd at the local community theater in the pine barrens of southern New Jersey. The newspaper says that they are looking for a few kids to play street urchins and I am determined to be one of those kids.

My grandfather William Patrick Dunbar has spent weeks coaching me on my audition song: "Cabaret." Pop Pop is an Atlantic City cop has the gentle spirit of Bing Crosby of White Christmas. Unlike my father who is prone to frightening rage, I hardly ever see Pop Pop angry, but he is fiercely protective of my mother and us children. A family story goes that once when I am about three I am dancing around the house telling everyone that I want to be a ballet dancer.

FAMILY MEMBER: "No Dougie, you don't want to be a ballet

dancer. Ya wanna be a policeman or a fireman!"

Everyone chimes in, except for my grandfather. His face gets red. He stands up from his favorite chair and says:

POP POP: "If my grandson wants to be a ballet dancer, He'll be a ballet dancer. And you's all will sit in the front row."

He loves music and has a beautiful baritone singing to my grandmother.

POP POP (singing): "Everybody loves somebody sometime".

Pop Pop has coached me on my song a million times, and I am ready to go to the audition. I am wearing a wild African print Dashiki that I buy with money I earn selling magazine subscriptions. My hair has been cut by Ginny at Sheer Delight Unisex Hair Stylists on Route 9 and I am growing a full on 'Fro that I maintain with a Black Afro pic in the shape of a raised fist. Ungula!

Riding my green and yellow Sears Stingray 3 speed through town, I am surprised, embarrassed, and sort of thrilled by the attention I am receiving from the very white, blue-collar community we live in. When Mr. Hamel sees me riding down the street, clutching my sheet music against the handlebars with streamers and African sleeves trailing in the wind, he throws down his rake and runs to his front door:

MR. HAMEL: "Honey! Kids, get out here quick. Wait until you see what the hell Dougie is wearing today. Don't ride so fast, lardo, you're going to get a heart attack. And Dougie … get a bra! Ha ha!"

My first audition is also the first time I have ever been in a theater. Though I have never seen a play, I have read all of Tennessee

Williams and have dreamt about Broadway incessantly.

The Atlantic Community Theater is a musty old playhouse with a tiny lobby and sixty raked movie house seats on either side of a center aisle. The stage is bare except for a piano and some theatrical lights that are focused on the floor.

When my name is called, I move, frozen with terror onto the tiny stage under the lights in front of all of the child and adult auditioners.

DOUGIE (singing through terror): "What good is sitting alone in your room? Time for a holiday. Life is a cabaret, old chum only a cabaret. Come taste the wine. Come hear the band. (becoming more confident) Come blow your horn start celebrating, right this way your table's waiting. What good's permitting some prophet of doom to wipe every smile away? (selling it for all he is worth) Life is a cabaret, old chum! Only a cabaret. And I love a Cab-ba-a-ret!"

I get cast as one of the urchins and discovering The Theatre sets my destiny spinning and introduces me to something that I become convinced I cannot ever dare live without: an audience.

ACKNOWLEDGMENTS

We thank Nancy Manocherian's the cell, which supported Read650 at its inception. A twenty-first century salon in the heart of New York City, their mission is to support the arts and incubate new works, and the cell made its beautiful performance space available to Read650 as we were finding our way. The cell: To mine the mind, pierce the heart, and awaken the soul.
TheCellTheatre.org

Artists Without Walls was created to inspire, uplift, and unite people and communities of diverse cultures through the pursuit of artistic achievement, and has supported and encouraged Read650 from its beginnings. Artists Without Walls: No Limits. No Walls. No Boundaries.
ArtistsWithoutWalls.com

We're grateful for the support and encouragement from The Writing Institute at Sarah Lawrence College, which supplies a steady stream of excellent writers to Read650. The Writing Institute helps writers in all genres progress and grow in their craft and welcomes them all into a very supportive community.
SarahLawrence.edu

READ650.COM

INFO @READ650.COM
FACEBOOK.COM/READ650